Making It i

A Practical Guide to Living in New York

Book Written By
Cornelius Raymond

This book is intended to provide practical advice
and information on living in New York City. The
author and publisher make no representations or
warranties with respect to the accuracy or
completeness of the contents of this book and
specifically disclaim any implied warranties of
merchantability or fitness for a particular purpose.
The advice and strategies contained herein may
not be suitable for every situation. The reader
should consult with a professional where
appropriate.

Table Of Content

Chapter 1: Introduction - Welcome to New York

New York City is one of the most exciting and vibrant cities in the world. It is home to over 8 million people and attracts millions of visitors each year. Whether you are moving to the city to start a new job, to attend school, or simply to experience everything that the city has to offer, there are many things you need to know to make your transition to life in New York as smooth as possible.

This chapter will provide an overview of what you can expect when moving to New York and introduce you to some of the key elements of the city that you will need to navigate as you begin your new life here.

Section 1.1: The Big Apple - What You Need to Know

In this section, we will explore some of the key facts and figures about New York City. We will look at the city's geography, climate, and population, as well as the many neighborhoods and communities that make up this great city.

New York City is located in the southeastern part of New York State, on the East Coast of the United States. It is made up of five boroughs: Manhattan,

Brooklyn, Queens, the Bronx, and Staten Island. Manhattan is the most densely populated borough and is home to many of the city's most famous landmarks, such as Central Park, the Empire State Building, and the Broadway theater district. Brooklyn, which is the most populous borough, is known for its diverse neighborhoods and thriving arts and culture scene.

The city has a humid subtropical climate, with hot summers and cold winters. The summers can be quite hot and humid, with temperatures often reaching 90 degrees Fahrenheit or higher. The winters can be cold and snowy, with temperatures sometimes dropping below freezing. It is important to be prepared for these weather conditions and to dress accordingly.

The population of New York City is over 8 million people, making it the most populous city in the United States. The city is incredibly diverse, with people from all over the world living and working in various neighborhoods and communities. This diversity is reflected in the city's many languages, cultures, and cuisines, making it a truly unique and exciting place to live.

Section 1.2: The Cost of Living in New York

One of the most important things you need to know about living in New York is that it can be an expensive city. In this section, we will explore some of the costs associated with living in the city, including housing, food, and transportation, and provide some tips on how to budget your money effectively.

Living in New York City can be expensive, with the cost of living significantly higher than the national average. One of the biggest expenses is housing, with rent prices often higher than in other parts of the country. However, many neighborhoods in the city offer more affordable options, and it is possible to find a good deal with some research and patience.

Other expenses to consider include food, transportation, and entertainment. The cost of groceries and eating out in New York can be higher than in other cities, but there are also many affordable options available, such as food trucks, delis, and street vendors. The city's public transit system is extensive and affordable, with a single ride on the subway or bus costing $2.75. Entertainment options can also vary in price, with some museums and galleries offering free admission and others charging entrance fees.

It is important to budget carefully when living in New York City and to be aware of the various expenses you will face. However, with some planning and creativity, it is possible to live in the city on a budget.

Section 1.3: Getting Around in New York

New York is a large and sprawling city, and getting around can be a challenge, especially if you are new to the area. In this section, we will explore the various transportation options available in the city, including the subway, buses, taxis, and other forms of public transit.

New York City is known for its extensive public transit system, which includes the subway, buses, and commuter trains. The subway is the most popular way to get around the city, with 24-hour service and extensive coverage throughout the five boroughs. The bus system is also extensive and can be a good option for traveling to areas not covered by the subway. Taxis and ride-sharing services like Uber and Lyft are also widely available in the city, although they can be more expensive than public transit.

It is important to be aware of the various transit options and to plan your routes carefully, especially when traveling during rush hour or to areas with heavy traffic. The MTA website and app can be helpful resources for planning your trips and checking service updates.

Section 1.4: Making the Most of Your Time in New York

New York is home to some of the world's most famous landmarks and attractions, as well as a thriving arts and culture scene. In this section, we will explore some of the best things to do and see in the city, from visiting the Statue of Liberty and the Empire State Building to attending Broadway shows and exploring the city's many museums and galleries.

New York City is home to a wide range of cultural attractions and entertainment options. Some of the most popular landmarks and attractions include the Statue of Liberty, Central Park, the Empire State Building, the Metropolitan Museum of Art, and the 9/11 Memorial and Museum. Broadway shows and off-Broadway theaters offer a diverse range of performances, from musicals to plays, and the city's many museums and galleries showcase art and artifacts from around the world.

Section 1.5: Conclusion

Moving to New York can be an exciting and challenging experience, but with the right preparation and knowledge, you can make the most of everything this great city has to offer. In this chapter, we have provided an overview of some of the key elements of life in New York, from its geography and climate to its transportation options and cultural attractions. In the chapters that follow, we will delve deeper into these topics and provide more detailed guidance on how to make the most of your life in the city.

Chapter 2: Finding a Place to Live in New York City

One of the most important things to consider when moving to New York City is finding a place to live. The city offers a wide variety of housing options, from high-rise apartments to brownstones to shared living spaces. In this chapter, we will explore the different types of housing available, as well as tips for finding the right place for you.

Section 2.1: Types of Housing in New York City

There are several types of housing available in New York City, including apartments, co-ops, and condos.

Apartments are the most common type of housing in the city and come in various sizes and styles. They can be found in high-rise buildings, walk-up buildings, or converted townhouses. Most apartments in the city are rented, and rental prices can vary widely depending on the neighborhood and the size and quality of the apartment.

Co-ops are another option for those looking to buy property in the city. A co-op is a type of housing where residents own shares in the building or complex, rather than owning their units. Co-ops often have stricter rules and regulations than other types of housing, and potential buyers must be approved by the co-op board before being allowed to purchase a unit.

Condos are similar to co-ops in that they are individually owned units within a larger building or complex. However, condo owners have more flexibility and control over their units than co-op owners, and there are generally fewer restrictions on renting or selling the unit.

Section 2.2: Neighborhoods in New York City

New York City is made up of five boroughs and hundreds of neighborhoods, each with its unique character and vibe. When looking for a place to live in the city, it is important to consider which neighborhood will best suit your needs and lifestyle.

Some popular neighborhoods for young professionals include Williamsburg in Brooklyn, the Lower East Side in Manhattan, and Astoria in Queens. These neighborhoods offer a vibrant arts and culture scene, as well as a variety of restaurants, bars, and nightlife options.

Families may prefer to live in neighborhoods like Park Slope in Brooklyn, Forest Hills in Queens, or the Upper West Side in Manhattan. These areas offer access to good schools and family-friendly activities, as well as plenty of parks and green spaces.

Section 2.3: Tips for Finding a Place to Live

Finding the right place to live in New York City can be a daunting task, but several tips and resources can make the process easier.

One of the best resources for finding an apartment or other types of housing is online listings, such as Craigslist or StreetEasy. These sites allow you to search for apartments based on your preferences and budget and often include photos and detailed descriptions of the units.

It is also a good idea to work with a real estate agent, especially if you are new to the city or unfamiliar with the different neighborhoods. A knowledgeable agent can help you find properties that meet your needs and budget, as well as provide guidance on the buying or renting process.

Finally, it is important to do your research and be prepared for the competitive nature of the New York City housing market. Apartments can be rented or sold quickly, so it is important to act fast if you find a place you like. It is also a good idea to have all your documents and finances in order before starting your search, as many landlords and co-op boards require extensive documentation and financial information from potential renters or buyers.

Section 2.4: Renting vs. Buying in New York City

Deciding whether to rent or buy in New York City can be a difficult decision. There are advantages and disadvantages to both options, and the right choice for you will depend on your circumstances and financial situation.

Renting is a popular option for many people who move to New York City, especially those who are new to the city or who are not ready to commit to a long-term investment. Renting allows for more flexibility and mobility, as well as the ability to avoid some of the costs and responsibilities associated with homeownership, such as property taxes and maintenance.

However, renting in New York City can be expensive, and the competition for apartments can be fierce. Many landlords require extensive documentation and financial information from potential renters, and it can be challenging to find an apartment in a desirable neighborhood that fits your budget.

Buying a home in New York City is a long-term investment that can provide stability and financial benefits over time. Property values in the city have historically increased over time, and owning a home can provide tax benefits and the ability to build equity over time.

However, buying a home in New York City can be very expensive, and the process can be complicated and time-consuming. Co-op boards often have strict rules and regulations, and the closing process can take several months to complete.

Finding a place to live in New York City can be challenging, but with some research and preparation, it is possible to find a home that meets your needs and budget. Whether you choose to rent or buy, and which neighborhood you choose to live in, will depend on a variety of factors, including your lifestyle, budget, and personal preferences.

Section 2.5: Conclusion

Finding a place to live in New York City can be a challenging but rewarding experience. By exploring the different types of housing available, researching neighborhoods, and considering the pros and cons of renting versus buying, you can make an informed decision that meets your needs and budget.

Whether you are a young professional looking for a vibrant, trendy neighborhood or a family looking for a peaceful, family-friendly community, New York City has something to offer for everyone. By following the tips and resources outlined in this chapter, you can navigate the competitive New

York City housing market and find a place to call home.

Chapter 3: Navigating Public Transit: Getting Around the City

One of the defining features of life in New York City is the extensive public transit system. From the iconic yellow cabs to the sprawling subway system, there are a variety of options for getting around the city. However, navigating public transit in New York City can be overwhelming, especially for newcomers. This chapter will provide an overview of the various transportation options available in the city, as well as tips and tricks for making the most of them.

Section 3.1: The Subway System

The New York City subway system is the backbone of the city's public transit system, providing access to all five boroughs and a variety of destinations. With over 470 stations and 24 different lines, it can be intimidating for first-time riders. However, with a little practice, the subway can be an efficient and cost-effective way to get around the city.

In this section, we will cover the basics of using the subway system, including purchasing a MetroCard, reading the subway map, and navigating transfers and connections. We will also provide tips for avoiding peak hours, staying safe while riding the subway, and making the most of your commute.

Here are some tips for avoiding peak hours on the New York City subway system:

1 Plan ahead: Check the MTA's website or use a transit app to see the busiest times on the subway. Avoid these peak hours whenever possible.

2 Leave early or late: If you can, adjust your schedule to leave for work or appointments earlier or later than the typical rush hour times. This can help you avoid the crowds and find a seat on the subway.

3 Consider alternate routes: Sometimes taking a less popular route can help you avoid crowded trains and stations. Use a transit app to explore different subway lines and routes to find the best option for your commute.

4 Take express trains: If available, taking an express train can help you avoid stops and crowds on local trains. However, be aware that express trains may not stop at all stations, so make sure to check the schedule before boarding.

5 Walk or bike: If you have a short distance to travel, consider walking or biking instead of taking the subway. This can not only help you avoid peak

hours, but also provide some exercise and fresh air.

Section 3.2: Buses

While the subway system is the most popular mode of public transit in New York City, the bus system is also an important and useful way to get around. With over 300 routes and thousands of stops throughout the city, buses can be a convenient option for getting to destinations not serviced by the subway.

In this section, we will cover the basics of using the bus system, including purchasing a MetroCard, reading the bus schedule, and navigating the different types of buses. We will also provide tips for planning your bus route, staying safe while riding the bus, and making the most of your trip.

Here are some tips for planning your bus route in New York City:

1 Use online resources: The MTA website provides a trip planner tool that allows you to enter your starting point, destination, and preferred travel time, and will generate a customized route for you. There are also several third-party apps that can help you plan your bus route, including Citymapper and Google Maps.

2 Check the schedule: Buses in New York City run on a fixed schedule, so it's important to check the schedule in advance to make sure you don't miss your bus. Schedules can be found at bus stops or online.

3 Know your stops: Make sure you know the name of the stop where you need to get off the bus. Some bus stops have multiple routes, so it's important to look for the specific route number you need.

4 Look for landmarks: If you're not familiar with the area, it can be helpful to look for landmarks near your destination. This can help you determine when to get off the bus and which direction to walk.

5 Be aware of bus-only lanes: In some areas, buses have their own dedicated lanes, which can help them move more quickly through traffic. Make sure you stay out of these lanes if you're not on a bus, and be aware that you may need to cross these lanes to get to your bus stop.

Section 3.3: Taxis and Ride-Sharing Services

In addition to public transit, New York City is also known for its iconic yellow taxis and the growing popularity of ride-sharing services like Uber and Lyft. While these options can be more expensive than public transit, they can also be more convenient and comfortable for certain trips.

In this section, we will cover the basics of using taxis and ride-sharing services, including pricing, safety tips, and the pros and cons of each option. We will also provide tips for finding a taxi or ride-sharing service, making the most of your ride, and avoiding common scams and pitfalls.

Here are some tips for finding a taxi or ride-sharing service in New York City:

1 Use a reliable app: When using a ride-sharing service, make sure to download a reliable app such as Uber or Lyft. These apps will allow you to easily and safely request a ride, track your driver's location, and pay for your trip.

2 Check for surge pricing: During peak hours or events, ride-sharing services may have surge pricing, which means that fares can be significantly higher. Check the app for any surge pricing notifications before requesting a ride.

3 Look for licensed taxis: If you prefer to take a traditional taxi, look for licensed yellow taxis with a medallion on the hood. You can also use the official NYC Taxi and Limousine Commission (TLC) app to hail a taxi and pay for your ride.

4 Check for wheelchair accessibility: If you require a wheelchair-accessible taxi or ride-sharing service,

check the app or service website for availability and accessibility options.

5 Be aware of scams: Be cautious of scams, such as unlicensed drivers or drivers who ask for payment outside of the app. Always confirm the driver's identity and vehicle information before getting into the car, and only pay through the app.

6 Know the tipping policy: Tipping is generally expected for taxis and ride-sharing services in New York City. Check the app or service website for their tipping policy, and consider tipping your driver for good service

Section 3.4: Accessibility

While New York City's public transit system is extensive and well-connected, it can be challenging for individuals with disabilities or mobility issues. Many subway stations are not wheelchair accessible, and buses can be crowded and difficult to navigate for those with physical limitations.

In this section, we will provide an overview of the accessibility options available in the city, including Access-A-Ride, a shared-ride paratransit service that provides transportation for individuals with disabilities. We will also provide tips and resources for planning accessible trips, finding wheelchair-accessible subway stations and buses, and making the most of your travels in the city.

Here are some tips and resources for planning accessible trips in New York City:

1 Use Access-A-Ride: Access-A-Ride is a shared-ride paratransit service that provides transportation for individuals with disabilities. You can make reservations online or by phone, and rides can be scheduled in advance or on-demand.

2 Plan ahead: When using public transit, plan your trip in advance to ensure that you are aware of any accessibility issues or potential barriers. Check the MTA's website or use an app like Transit or Google Maps to find wheelchair-accessible subway stations and bus routes.

3 Know your rights: Under the Americans with Disabilities Act (ADA), public transportation providers are required to provide equal access and reasonable accommodations for individuals with disabilities. If you encounter any issues or have concerns about accessibility, don't hesitate to speak up and advocate for yourself.

4 Use assistive technology: There are a variety of assistive technology tools available to help individuals with disabilities navigate the city, such as audio-based navigation apps, screen readers, and captioning services.

5 Seek out resources: There are many resources available to help individuals with disabilities navigate the city, such as the Mayor's Office for People with Disabilities and the Disability Rights Advocates. These organizations can provide information and support for planning accessible trips and navigating public transit

3.5: Apps and Resources

In today's digital age, there are a variety of apps and resources available to help navigate public transit in New York City. From real-time transit tracking to trip planning and fare calculators, these tools can be invaluable for getting around the city.

In this section, we will provide an overview of some of the most popular and useful apps and resources for navigating public transit in New York City, including the MTA's official app, Transit, Google Maps, and Citymapper. We will also provide tips for using these apps and resources effectively, as well as additional resources for staying up-to-date on changes and delays in the transit system.

Here are some tips for using these apps and resources effectively:

1 Familiarize yourself with the app: Take the time to explore and learn how to use the features of the app. This will help you navigate the transit system more efficiently.

2 Use real-time data: Many of these apps offer real-time data on transit schedules and delays. Check this information before you leave, so you can plan accordingly and avoid waiting unnecessarily.

3 Set alerts: Most transit apps allow you to set alerts for delays, service changes, and other important information. Make sure to set up alerts for your regular routes, so you can stay informed about any changes or delays.

4 Check multiple apps: While some apps may have more comprehensive information than others, it's always a good idea to check multiple apps to confirm transit information and ensure accuracy.

Section 3.6: Sustainable Transportation

As New York City continues to grow and develop, there is increasing emphasis on sustainable transportation options, such as biking, walking, and electric scooters. These modes of transportation can be an eco-friendly and cost-effective alternative to traditional public transit.

In this section, we will provide an overview of the sustainable transportation options available in New York City, including the Citi Bike bike-share program, electric scooters, and walking routes. We will also provide tips for staying safe and following the rules of the road while using these modes of transportation.

New York City offers a variety of sustainable transportation options, which are becoming increasingly popular due to their environmental and economic benefits. One popular option is the Citi Bike bike-share program, which has thousands of bikes available throughout the city for short-term rentals. Additionally, electric scooters are becoming more common in certain areas of the city, offering a convenient and eco-friendly way to travel short distances. Walking is also a great way to get around, with numerous pedestrian-friendly areas and parks throughout the city. For longer distances, the subway and bus systems also offer some sustainable options, with an increasing number of electric and hybrid vehicles in use. To ensure safe and responsible use of these transportation options, it's important to follow the rules of the road, wear proper safety gear, and be aware of surrounding pedestrians and vehicles

Here are some tips for staying safe and following the rules of the road while using sustainable transportation options in New York City:

1 Wear protective gear: If you're biking or using an electric scooter, always wear a helmet and any other appropriate protective gear, such as knee or elbow pads.

2 Follow traffic laws: Bicyclists and scooter riders must follow the same traffic laws as motor vehicles. This includes stopping at stop signs and red lights, yielding to pedestrians, and using hand signals to indicate turns.

3 Stay visible: When biking or walking, wear bright or reflective clothing, especially if you are traveling at night. Use lights or reflectors to make yourself visible to motorists and other riders.

4 Be aware of your surroundings: Pay attention to your surroundings and be aware of potential hazards such as potholes, debris, or other obstacles. Also, be aware of other riders and pedestrians who may be sharing the road or sidewalk with you.

5 Use designated bike lanes: Use designated bike lanes whenever possible, and avoid riding on busy roads or highways.

6 Plan your route: Plan your route ahead of time and try to choose quieter, less congested roads. You can use online maps or smartphone apps to help plan your route and find bike lanes or dedicated walking paths.

7 Follow parking rules: When using bike-share programs or parking your bike or scooter, make sure to follow the designated parking rules and not block sidewalks or pedestrian walkways.

By following these tips, you can help ensure your safety while using sustainable transportation options in New York City.

Navigating public transit in New York City can be intimidating, but with a little practice and preparation, it can be a convenient and cost-effective way to get around the city. By understanding the basics of the subway system, buses, taxis, and ride-sharing services, you can choose the best option for your needs and budget. By following the tips and resources outlined in this chapter, you can make the most of your travels in a city that never sleeps.

Section 3.7: Conclusion

Navigating public transit in New York City can be a challenge, but with the right tools and resources, it can be a convenient and efficient way to get around the city. By understanding the basics of the subway system, buses, taxis, and ride-sharing services, as well as accessibility options and sustainable transportation alternatives, you can choose the best option for your needs and budget. By following the tips and resources outlined in this chapter, you can make the most of your travels in a city that never sleeps.

Chapter 4: Apartment Hunting: How to Find Your Dream Apartment

New York City is known for its unique architecture and diverse neighborhoods, each offering a different vibe and style of living. Whether you're moving to the city for the first time or looking for a new place to call home, apartment hunting can be an exciting and daunting process. In this chapter, we will provide an overview of the apartment-hunting process and offer tips for finding your dream apartment.

Section 4.1: Determining Your Budget

Before beginning your apartment search, it's important to determine your budget. New York City is known for its high cost of living, so it's essential to set realistic expectations and prioritize your needs. In this section, we will provide tips for setting a budget and understanding the costs associated with renting an apartment in New York City, including rent, utilities, and broker fees.

here are some tips for setting a budget and understanding the costs associated with renting an apartment in New York City:

1 Assess your income: The first step in setting a budget is to assess your income. Determine how much you can realistically afford to spend on rent each month.

2 Calculate your expenses: Calculate all of your monthly expenses, including utilities, transportation costs, food, and entertainment. This will help you determine how much money you have left over to spend on rent.

3 Consider your lifestyle: Consider your lifestyle and prioritize your needs. Do you need a spacious apartment with all the amenities, or are you willing to compromise on space for a more affordable rent?

4 Research rental prices: Research the average rental prices in your preferred neighborhoods to get an idea of what to expect. Keep in mind that prices can vary depending on the location, amenities, and size of the apartment.

5 Factor in broker fees: In New York City, it's common to use a broker to help you find an apartment. Be aware that brokers typically charge a fee, which is usually equal to one month's rent.

6 Budget for utilities: Be sure to budget for utilities, including electricity, gas, and water. These costs can add up quickly, especially during the winter months when heating bills can be high.

7 Be prepared for unexpected expenses: Unexpected expenses can arise when renting an apartment, such as repairs or maintenance costs. Be sure to budget for these expenses as well.

By following these tips, you can set a realistic budget and understand the costs associated with renting an apartment in New York City.

Section 4.2: Choosing Your Neighborhood

New York City is home to over 8 million people, with a vast array of neighborhoods to choose from. Each neighborhood has its unique character and amenities, so it's important to choose a neighborhood that aligns with your lifestyle and needs. In this section, we will provide an overview of some of the most popular neighborhoods in the city, along with information about their demographics, amenities, and accessibility.

here's an overview of some of the most popular neighborhoods in New York City:

1 Manhattan: As the most densely populated borough in the city, Manhattan offers an array of neighborhoods, each with their unique personality. It's a center of finance, culture, and shopping, and is home to iconic landmarks like the Empire State Building, Central Park, and Times Square.

2 Brooklyn: Known for its hipster vibe, Brooklyn has become an increasingly popular place to live in recent years. It offers a more relaxed, community-driven atmosphere than Manhattan, with numerous parks, restaurants, and art galleries.

3 Queens: As the largest borough by land area, Queens is one of the most ethnically diverse areas in the country, and offers a range of cultural attractions, including the Queens Museum and the New York Hall of Science. It's also home to several major airports and sports arenas.

4 The Bronx: The northernmost borough in the city, The Bronx is a culturally rich area with a mix of residential and commercial areas. It's home to the New York Botanical Garden, the Bronx Zoo, and Yankee Stadium.

5 Staten Island: The least populous borough, Staten Island is known for its suburban feel and more laid-back lifestyle. It's a great choice for those seeking a quieter atmosphere, while still being able to enjoy access to the city through the Staten Island Ferry

Section 4.3: Starting Your Search

Once you've determined your budget and chosen your preferred neighborhoods, it's time to start your apartment search. In this section, we will provide an overview of the different types of apartments available in New York City, including studio, one-bedroom, and two-bedroom apartments, as well as lofts and townhouses. We will also discuss the various ways to find available apartments, including online listings, broker services, and word-of-mouth.

Here are the most common types of apartments available in the city:

1 Studio Apartments: These apartments consist of a single open space, which typically includes a bedroom, living area, and kitchenette, all in one room. Studio apartments are ideal for single individuals or couples who want to live in the city on a budget.

2 One-Bedroom Apartments: These apartments consist of a separate bedroom and a living area, along with a kitchen and bathroom. One-bedroom apartments are ideal for individuals or couples who want more space and privacy than a studio apartment.

3 Two-Bedroom Apartments: These apartments offer two separate bedrooms, a living area, a kitchen, and a bathroom. Two-bedroom apartments are ideal for families or roommates who want more space and privacy.

4 Lofts: Lofts are large open spaces that were once industrial or commercial buildings, converted into

residential units. They often feature high ceilings, exposed brick, and other unique architectural elements.

5 Townhouses: These are multi-story buildings that offer several bedrooms, bathrooms, and living areas. They provide more space and privacy than apartments and are ideal for larger families.

Each of these apartment types offers unique features and benefits, and the one you choose will depend on your personal preferences and needs.

Here are several ways to find available apartments in New York City.

1 Online listings: There are many websites that offer listings of available apartments in the city, such as StreetEasy, Zillow, and Apartments.com. These websites allow you to search for apartments based on location, price, and other preferences.

2 Broker services: Many apartment seekers in New York City use the services of a real estate broker to help them find an apartment. Brokers have access to exclusive listings and can help you navigate the rental process, but they typically charge a fee of 10-15% of the annual rent.

3 Word-of-mouth: Don't underestimate the power of asking around. Let your friends, family, and coworkers know that you're looking for an

apartment, and you might be surprised at the leads you get.

4 Walking around: Sometimes the best way to find an apartment is to simply walk around the neighborhood you want to live in and look for "For Rent" signs in windows or on bulletin boards.

No matter which method you choose, be prepared to act quickly. The rental market in New York City moves fast, so be ready to submit an application and deposit as soon as you find an apartment you like.

Section 4.4: Touring Apartments

Once you've found potential apartments, it's important to schedule tours to see them in person. In this section, we will provide tips for scheduling and preparing for apartment tours, including what to look for during your visit and how to ask the right questions.

Here are some tips for scheduling and preparing for apartment tours:

1 Schedule tours in advance: Make sure to schedule tours with the landlord or leasing agent in advance to ensure availability and avoid wasting time.

2 Prepare a list of questions: Before the tour, prepare a list of questions to ask the landlord or leasing agent. This can include questions about the lease, move-in requirements, building amenities, and more.

3 Take notes: Bring a notepad and pen to take notes during the tour. This will help you remember important details about each apartment you visit.

4 Check for damages: Look for any damages or issues in the apartment, such as holes in the walls, leaks, or broken appliances. Make sure to take photos or videos of any issues to reference later.

5 Consider the neighborhood: When touring an apartment, also take the time to explore the surrounding neighborhood. Consider factors like proximity to public transportation, nearby restaurants and shops, and overall safety.

6 Visualize your life in the space: As you tour each apartment, try to envision yourself living there. Consider whether the space would fit your lifestyle and needs, and whether you could see yourself being happy there.

By following these tips, you can make the most of your apartment tours and find the right apartment for you.

Section 4.5: Applying for an Apartment

After finding your dream apartment, the next step is to apply. In this section, we will provide an overview of the application process, including what documents and information you'll need to provide, how to negotiate the terms of your lease, and how to prepare for a credit check.

The application process for renting an apartment in New York City typically involves providing personal and financial information to the landlord or management company.

Here's an overview of the steps involved:

1 Gather necessary documents: Before you begin the application process, you will need to gather important documents such as proof of employment, recent pay stubs, and a photo ID. You may also need to provide references, such as previous landlords or personal references.

2 Fill out an application: Once you have gathered all the necessary information, you will need to fill out an application provided by the landlord or management company. The application will typically ask for your personal and employment information, as well as your rental history and financial information.

3 Submit your application: After completing the application, you will need to submit it to the landlord or management company, along with any necessary fees. Depending on the landlord or management company, you may be required to pay an application fee or provide a deposit at this stage.

4 Wait for approval: The landlord or management company will review your application and may conduct a background or credit check. This process may take several days, and you should be prepared to provide additional information if requested.

5 Negotiate lease terms: Once you are approved, the landlord or management company will provide you with a lease agreement. You may have the opportunity to negotiate the terms of the lease, such as the length of the lease, move-in date, or rent amount.

6 Sign the lease: Once you have agreed to the terms of the lease, you will need to sign it and provide any required deposits or fees. The landlord or management company will provide you with a copy of the lease for your records.

It's important to remember that the application process may vary depending on the landlord or management company, so it's always a good idea to ask for clarification if you have any questions.

Section 4.6: Moving In

Congratulations, you've found your dream apartment! Now it's time to start the moving process. In this section,we will provide tips for a smooth move-in process, including how to hire a moving company, how to pack efficiently, and how to address any potential issues with the apartment before moving in.

Tips for a smooth move in process

1 Hire a reputable moving company: Research and choose a reliable moving company that can handle your move efficiently and securely. Get referrals from friends and family, read online reviews, and make sure they are licensed and insured.

2 Plan your move ahead of time: Start planning your move well in advance to avoid any last-minute stress. Book your moving company as early as possible and make a checklist of all the tasks that need to be done before the move.

3 Pack efficiently: Packing can be a daunting task, but it's essential to do it efficiently to avoid damage to your belongings during the move. Use high-quality boxes and packing materials, label each box with the contents and room it belongs to, and make sure to pack fragile items with extra care.

4 Check your new apartment for any issues: Before moving in, inspect your new apartment for any issues, such as leaks, cracks, or damages. Take photos and document any problems to bring them to the attention of your landlord or property manager.

5 Make arrangements for utilities and services: Arrange for utilities such as gas, electricity, and internet to be connected before you move in. This will help you settle in smoothly and avoid any inconvenience or unexpected charges.

6 Clean your new apartment: It's always a good idea to clean your new apartment before moving in, so you can start fresh in a clean and comfortable space. If you are not able to do it yourself, consider hiring a professional cleaning service.

By following these tips, you can make your move-in process smoother and stress-free, allowing you to settle into your new apartment and start enjoying your life in New York City

Section 4.7: Dealing with Landlords and Building Management

While living in an apartment, it's important to have a good relationship with your landlord and building management. In this section, we will provide tips for maintaining a positive relationship with them, including paying rent on time, reporting any maintenance issues promptly, and being a respectful tenant.

Section 4.8: Subletting and Roommates

Sometimes circumstances may require you to sublet your apartment or find a roommate to share the cost of living. In this section, we will provide information on subletting laws and regulations in New York City, as well as tips for finding and living with a roommate.

Section 4.9: Understanding Lease Renewals and Terminations

Lease renewals and terminations are a normal part of apartment living. In this section, we will provide information on lease renewal and termination laws and regulations in New York City, as well as tips for negotiating lease terms and handling the move-out process.

Here are some tips for negotiating lease terms and handling the move-out process:

1 Start early: If you're thinking about renewing or terminating your lease, start the process as early as possible. This will give you plenty of time to negotiate with your landlord and make any necessary arrangements.

2 Review your lease: Before negotiating with your landlord, review your lease agreement and make sure you understand all the terms and conditions. This will help you make an informed decision and negotiate effectively.

3 Communicate effectively: When negotiating with your landlord, make sure to communicate clearly and respectfully. Clearly state your needs and concerns, and listen to their perspective as well.

4 Consider the market: Before negotiating lease terms, research the current rental market in your area. This will give you an idea of the average rent prices and help you negotiate a fair deal.

5 Handle move-out properly: If you decide to move out, make sure to give your landlord proper notice and follow all necessary procedures for returning keys, getting your security deposit back, and cleaning the apartment. This will help ensure a smooth and stress-free move-out process.

By following these tips, you can effectively negotiate lease terms and handle the move-out process with confidence and ease.

Section 4.10: Coping with Rent Increases

Rent increases are a common occurrence in New York City, but there are ways to cope with them. In this section, we will provide tips for negotiating rent increases, understanding your lease terms, and finding alternative living arrangements if necessary.

Here are some tips for negotiating rent increases:

1 Be informed: Before negotiating, research the current market rates in your area to ensure that you have a fair understanding of what rent prices should be.

2 Be proactive: Don't wait until the last minute to address a rent increase. Reach out to your landlord before the increase goes into effect, and try to negotiate a more reasonable price.

3 Show your value as a tenant: Highlight what a good tenant you have been, including always paying rent on time and maintaining the apartment. If you are a long-term tenant, emphasize your loyalty to the building.

4 Offer to renew your lease: If you're currently on a month-to-month lease, consider offering to sign a longer-term lease in exchange for a more reasonable rent increase.

5 Negotiate additional perks: If your landlord won't budge on the rent increase, see if you can negotiate other perks such as a new appliance or a renovation to the apartment.

Remember, always approach negotiations with a respectful and professional attitude, and be prepared to compromise.

Section 4.11: Apartment Security

Apartment security is essential for feeling safe and secure in your home. In this section, we will provide tips for securing your apartment, including installing a security system, reinforcing locks, and maintaining good relationships with your neighbors.

Tips For Securing Your Apartment

1 Install a security system: Consider installing a security system in your apartment that includes cameras, alarms, and motion detectors. This will provide an extra layer of protection and deter potential intruders.

2 Reinforce locks: Ensure that all locks on your doors and windows are secure and sturdy. Consider upgrading to deadbolts or adding a security bar to your sliding glass door.

3 Keep your keys secure: Don't leave your keys lying around or with neighbors you don't trust. Consider investing in a keyless entry system or a safe to store your spare keys.

4 Be aware of your surroundings: Take note of your surroundings and be cautious when entering and

leaving your building. Avoid letting strangers into the building, and report any suspicious behavior to the building management.

5 Maintain good relationships with your neighbors: Get to know your neighbors and maintain a positive relationship with them. This can help create a sense of community and increase overall safety in the building.

By following these tips, you can help ensure that your apartment is a safe and secure place to call home.

Section 4.12: Tips for Apartment Living in New York City

Living in an apartment in New York City can be a unique and exciting experience. In this section, we will provide tips for making the most of your apartment living experience, including how to decorate your apartment, how to deal with noisy neighbors, and how to enjoy all that the city has to offer while maintaining a comfortable and peaceful living space.

Tips for Apartment living in New York City

1 Make the most of your space: Apartments in New York City are often smaller than those in other cities, so it's important to maximize your space.

Consider using multi-functional furniture, such as a bed with built-in storage, to save space.

2 Decorate with care: Personalize your apartment to make it feel like home, but be mindful of your lease agreement. Avoid making permanent changes that could result in penalties or lost security deposits.

3 Be mindful of noise: Noise is a common issue in apartments, so be mindful of your own noise level and be considerate of your neighbors. If you have noisy neighbors, try talking to them about the issue or consider investing in soundproofing materials.

4 Keep your apartment clean: New York City is a bustling city with a lot of dirt and dust, so it's important to keep your apartment clean. Regular cleaning can help keep the air quality in your apartment healthy and pleasant.

5 Build community: Living in an apartment building can be an opportunity to build a sense of community with your neighbors. Consider hosting a potluck or game night in the common area to get to know your neighbors.

6 Stay safe: Be aware of potential safety hazards in your building, such as faulty wiring or unsecured entryways. Report any concerns to your landlord or property manager immediately.

7 Enjoy the city: Living in New York City means you have access to some of the world's best food, culture, and entertainment. Take advantage of everything the city has to offer, but remember to balance your social life with your need for a comfortable and peaceful living space.

In conclusion, apartment hunting in New York City can be an overwhelming process, but with the right tools and information, it can also be an exciting and rewarding experience. By understanding your budget, choosing the right neighborhood, starting your search, touring apartments, applying for an apartment, moving in, and maintaining a positive relationship with your landlord and building management, you can find and enjoy your dream apartment in the city that never sleeps.

Chapter 5: Managing Finances: Budgeting for New York City Living

Living in New York City can be expensive, but it doesn't have to be unaffordable. In this chapter, we will discuss how to manage your finances and create a budget that allows you to live comfortably in the city.

Section 5.1: Understanding the Cost of Living in New York City

Before creating a budget, it's important to understand the cost of living in New York City. In this section, we will provide an overview of the average costs of housing, transportation, food, and entertainment in the city, and how they may vary depending on where you live.

here is an overview of the average costs of living in New York City:

1 Housing: Rent prices can vary greatly depending on the neighborhood, size, and type of apartment. On average, a studio apartment can cost around $2,500 per month, while a one-bedroom apartment can cost around $3,000 to $4,000 per month. The

cost can go up significantly if you opt for a larger apartment or a more expensive neighborhood.

2 Transportation: The cost of transportation in New York City is also a significant expense. A monthly MetroCard, which gives you unlimited access to the subway and bus systems, costs around $127. If you prefer to use ride-sharing services like Uber or Lyft, the cost can add up quickly, especially during peak hours or busy times.

3 Food: New York City has a reputation for having some of the best food in the world, but eating out can be expensive. The average cost of a meal at a mid-range restaurant is around $20 to $30 per person, and prices can be much higher at high-end restaurants. Groceries can also be expensive, with a gallon of milk costing around $4 and a loaf of bread costing around $3.

4 Entertainment: New York City is known for its vibrant entertainment scene, with options for theater, music, sports, and more. However, attending events and activities can be costly. A ticket to a Broadway show can cost hundreds of dollars, while a professional sports game can cost over $100 per ticket.

Section 5.2: Assessing Your Income and Expenses

To create a realistic budget, you need to know how much money you're bringing in and how much you're spending. In this section, we will provide tips for assessing your income and expenses, including tracking your spending and identifying areas where you can cut back.

Here are some tips for assessing your income and expenses in New York City:

1 Calculate your monthly income: This should include your salary or wages, as well as any additional income streams you have.

2 Track your expenses: Use a budgeting app or create a spreadsheet to track your expenses for a few months. This will help you identify your spending habits and areas where you can cut back.

3 Create categories: Organize your expenses into categories such as housing, transportation, food, and entertainment. This will help you see where your money is going.

4 Determine your fixed expenses: These are expenses that stay the same each month, such as rent or a car payment.

5 Identify variable expenses: These are expenses that can vary from month to month, such as groceries or entertainment.

6 Prioritize your expenses: Determine which expenses are essential and which can be cut back. For example, while transportation may be essential, you can likely find ways to reduce your entertainment expenses.

7 Set goals: Once you've identified areas where you can cut back, set specific goals for reducing your spending in those areas. This will help you stay on track and save more money.

Section 5.3: Creating a Budget

With a clear understanding of your income and expenses, you can create a budget that works for you. In this section, we will provide tips for creating a budget, including setting financial goals, prioritizing expenses, and establishing an emergency fund.

Here are some tips for creating a budget:

1 Set financial goals: Determine your short-term and long-term financial goals, such as saving for a down payment on a home or paying off debt. This will help you prioritize your spending and make sure your budget is aligned with your overall financial objectives.

2 Categorize your expenses: Divide your expenses into categories, such as rent, utilities, groceries, entertainment, and transportation. This will help you

get a clear picture of where your money is going and identify areas where you can cut back.

3 Prioritize your expenses: Determine which expenses are essential and which are discretionary. Make sure you cover your essential expenses first, such as rent, utilities, and groceries, before spending money on discretionary items like eating out or buying new clothes.

4 Use a budgeting tool: There are many budgeting tools available, such as budgeting apps and spreadsheets, that can help you create and track your budget. Find one that works for you and use it consistently to stay on top of your finances.

5 Establish an emergency fund: Set aside a portion of your budget for unexpected expenses or emergencies, such as car repairs or medical bills. Having an emergency fund can help you avoid going into debt when unexpected expenses arise.

Section 5.4: Saving Money in New York City

Living in New York City doesn't have to mean sacrificing your savings. In this section, we will provide tips for saving money in the city, including taking advantage of free or low-cost activities, using public transportation, and cooking at home.

here are some tips for saving money in New York City:

1 Take advantage of free or low-cost activities: There are plenty of free and low-cost activities in New York City, such as visiting museums on their free admission days or attending outdoor concerts in the park.

2 Use public transportation: While owning a car in the city can be expensive, public transportation is relatively affordable and can save you money on gas, parking, and other car-related expenses. Consider getting a monthly unlimited metro card to save even more.

3 Cook at home: Eating out in New York City can be costly, but cooking at home can save you a lot of money. Try meal prepping for the week or shopping for groceries in bulk to save even more.

4 Shop smart: Look for deals and discounts when shopping for necessities, such as groceries and household items. Consider using cashback apps or discount codes to save money.

5 Negotiate bills: Negotiate with your service providers, such as cable and internet, to see if you can get a better deal or bundle your services for a lower price.

6 Find roommates: Sharing an apartment with roommates can help you split the cost of rent and utilities, making it more affordable to live in the city.

7 Take advantage of work perks: Many companies offer employee discounts or perks, such as gym memberships or transit benefits. Be sure to take advantage of these perks to save money.

Section 5.5: Managing Debt

Debt can be a major source of stress and can hinder your ability to save and achieve financial goals. In this section, we will provide tips for managing debt, including creating a debt repayment plan and negotiating with creditors.

Here are some tips for managing debt:

1 Create a budget: Before you can start paying off debt, it's important to know exactly how much money you have coming in and going out each month. Start by tracking your expenses and creating a budget that prioritizes debt repayment.

2 Prioritize high-interest debt: If you have multiple debts, start by focusing on the ones with the highest interest rates. This will help you save money in the long run and pay off your debts faster.

3 Negotiate with creditors: If you're struggling to make payments on your debt, consider contacting your creditors to negotiate a payment plan or lower interest rate. They may be willing to work with you if

they see that you're making an effort to pay off your debt.

4 Consider debt consolidation: If you have multiple debts with high interest rates, consolidating them into a single loan with a lower interest rate can help you save money and pay off your debt faster.

5 Look for ways to increase your income: If you're struggling to make payments on your debt, consider taking on a side hustle or finding ways to increase your income. This can help you pay off your debts faster and achieve your financial goals.

Section 5.6: Planning for the Future

While it's important to focus on the present, it's also important to plan for the future. In this section, we will provide tips for planning for the future, including saving for retirement, creating an estate plan, and purchasing insurance.

here are some tips for planning for the future:

1 Save for retirement: Start saving for retirement as soon as possible, even if you're only able to contribute a small amount each month. Take advantage of any employer-sponsored retirement plans or individual retirement accounts (IRAs) available to you.

2 Create an emergency fund: Set aside some money each month for unexpected expenses or emergencies. Experts recommend having enough saved to cover 3-6 months of living expenses.

3 Establish an estate plan: Create a will, trust, or other legal document outlining how you want your assets to be distributed after you pass away. This can also help ensure your loved ones are taken care of.

4 Purchase insurance: Protect yourself and your assets by purchasing insurance, such as health, auto, or renter's insurance. Make sure to shop around for the best rates and coverage.

5 Invest in your education and skills: Consider investing in your education and skills to improve your earning potential and job prospects in the future. This can include taking courses or workshops, earning a degree or certification, or learning a new skill.

Section 5.7: Resources for Financial Assistance

If you find yourself in financial need, there are resources available to help. In this section, we will provide information on resources for financial assistance, including government programs, non-profit organizations, and community services.

Here are some examples of resources for financial assistance in New York City:

1 NYC Department of Social Services: The department provides a range of services for low-income residents, including cash assistance, food stamps, and Medicaid.

2 NYC Housing Preservation and Development: The agency provides affordable housing opportunities and rental assistance programs.

3 Food Bank for New York City: The organization provides food to people in need through a network of food pantries and soup kitchens.

4 New York City Free Clinic: The clinic provides free medical care to uninsured and underinsured New Yorkers.

5 Financial Counseling: There are several non-profit organizations that offer free financial counseling and education services, such as the Financial Clinic and the Neighborhood Trust Financial Partners.

6 Legal Services NYC: The organization provides free legal services to low-income New Yorkers in a range of areas, including housing, public benefits, and debt.

7 NYC Small Business Services: The agency provides support to small businesses through training, financing, and technical assistance programs.

8 The Robin Hood Foundation: The organization funds a range of programs and initiatives aimed at fighting poverty in New York City, including job training and education programs.

Managing your finances in New York City requires careful planning and budgeting. By understanding the cost of living in the city, assessing your income and expenses, creating a budget, saving money, managing debt, planning for the future, and utilizing resources for financial assistance if needed, you can live comfortably and confidently in a city that never sleeps.

By following the tips in this chapter, you can effectively manage your finances and enjoy all that New York City has to offer without breaking the bank. It's important to remember that financial well-being is a process, and it takes time and effort to build a stable financial future. However, with patience, discipline, and a solid plan, you can achieve financial success in New York City and beyond.

Chapter 6: Employment: Finding a Job in the City

New York City is home to a diverse and thriving job market, with opportunities available in a wide range of industries. However, the competition for jobs can be fierce, so it's important to approach your job search with a strategic and proactive mindset. In this chapter, we'll explore the ins and outs of finding a job in the city, including:

6.1: Assessing Your Skills and Interests

Before you begin your job search, take some time to reflect on your skills and interests. Consider your education, work experience, and any other relevant qualifications you may have. Think about the type of work that interests you and the industries you would like to explore. This self-assessment will help you target your job search and make informed decisions about the positions you apply for.

6.2: Identifying Job Opportunities

There are many ways to identify job opportunities in New York City. Online job boards, such as Indeed, Glassdoor, and LinkedIn, are a great place to start. You can also explore industry-specific job boards or company websites for openings in your field. Networking is another valuable tool for finding job opportunities. Attend industry events and connect with professionals in your field to learn about potential job openings.

6.3: Crafting Your Resume and Cover Letter

Your resume and cover letter are your first impression with potential employers, so it's important to make them stand out. Tailor your resume and cover letter to each job you apply for, highlighting your relevant skills and experience. Be sure to proofread your documents carefully and have a trusted friend or mentor review them as well.

6.4: Navigating the Application Process

Once you've identified job opportunities and crafted your resume and cover letter, it's time to apply. Some job applications may require additional materials, such as a writing sample or references. Be sure to follow the application instructions carefully and submit all required materials.

6.5: Interviewing

If your application is successful, you may be invited to interview for the position. Prepare for your interview by researching the company and practicing your responses to common interview questions. Dress professionally and arrive on time. After the interview, be sure to follow up with a thank-you note or email.

6.6: Negotiating Salary and Benefits

If you receive a job offer, take some time to evaluate the salary and benefits package. Consider factors such as health insurance, retirement plans, and vacation time. You may be able to negotiate some aspects of the offer, so don't be afraid to ask for what you need.

6.7: Navigating Immigration and Work Authorization

For individuals who are not U.S. citizens, navigating the immigration and work authorization process can be an important part of finding employment in New York City. It's important to understand the different visa categories and work authorization options available, as well as any potential limitations or restrictions. Seek guidance from an immigration attorney or other qualified professional to ensure that you are taking the necessary steps to comply with U.S. immigration law.

6.8: Exploring Freelance and Gig Work

In addition to traditional full-time employment, there are many opportunities for freelance and gig work in New York City. Platforms such as Upwork, TaskRabbit, and Uber offer flexible work arrangements and the ability to set your schedule. However, it's important to carefully evaluate the risks and benefits of these types of work arrangements, as they may not offer the same level of stability and benefits as traditional employment.

6.9: Building a Professional Network

Building a professional network is an important part of finding employment and advancing your career in New York City. Attend industry events, join professional organizations, and connect with colleagues and mentors in your field. Networking can help you learn about job opportunities, gain valuable insights and advice, and build relationships that can support your career growth.

6.10: Continuing Your Education and Professional Development

Continuing education and professional development are key components of long-term career success in New York City. Consider pursuing advanced degrees or certifications in your field, attending conferences and workshops, and staying up-to-date on industry trends and best practices. Investing in your professional development can help you stay competitive in the job market and advance your career over time.

In summary, finding a job in New York City requires a strategic approach and a commitment to the job search process. By assessing your skills and interests, identifying job opportunities, crafting strong application materials, and preparing for interviews and negotiations, you can position yourself for success in the city's dynamic job market.

By following the tips in this chapter, you can approach your job search in New York City with confidence and focus. Whether you are seeking traditional employment, freelance work, or other types of opportunities, it's important to be proactive and strategic in your approach. With hard work and persistence, you can find a job that aligns with your skills and interests and supports your long-term career goals.

Chapter 7: Dining Out: Eating Your Way Through the City's Best Restaurants

One of the best things about living in New York City is the incredible food scene. From Michelin-starred restaurants to hole-in-the-wall joints, the city is a food lover's paradise. In this chapter, we'll explore some of the best restaurants in the city and provide tips on how to make the most of your dining experience.

7.1: Exploring Different Cuisines

New York City is a melting pot of cultures, and the food scene reflects that diversity. You can find virtually any type of cuisine in the city, from Italian and Chinese to Mexican and Ethiopian. Take the opportunity to explore different cuisines and expand your culinary horizons. Check out neighborhoods like Little Italy, Chinatown, and Jackson Heights to experience authentic ethnic cuisine.

7.2: Finding the Best Restaurants

With so many restaurants in the city, it can be overwhelming to decide where to eat. One of the best ways to discover new restaurants is by asking for recommendations from friends, colleagues, and locals. You can also consult food blogs, restaurant review websites like Yelp and Zagat, and social media platforms like Instagram.

7.3: Making Reservations

Many of the city's most popular restaurants require reservations, so it's important to plan. Make reservations as far in advance as possible, and be prepared to be flexible with your dining schedule. Some restaurants offer special prix-fixe menus during off-peak hours, so you may be able to score a great deal by dining early or late.

7.4: Navigating Restaurant Etiquette

New York City has a unique dining culture, and it's important to understand the unwritten rules of restaurant etiquette. For example, it's customary to tip 20% of the total bill, and it's considered rude to linger at the table after you've finished your meal. Dress codes vary depending on the restaurant, so be sure to check the dress code before you go.

7.5: Budgeting for Dining Out

Dining out can be expensive in New York City, but there are ways to enjoy great food without breaking the bank. Look for restaurants that offer special deals and promotions, such as prix-fixe menus and happy hour specials. You can also save money by dining during off-peak hours or exploring more affordable neighborhoods like the East Village and Williamsburg.

7.6: Trying New Foods

New York City is the perfect place to experiment with new foods and ingredients. Be adventurous and try dishes you've never had before, or ask the waiter for recommendations. You may discover a new favorite food or cuisine that you never would have tried otherwise.

7.7: Supporting Local Restaurants

In recent years, small businesses, including restaurants, have struggled to stay afloat in the face of increasing competition from chain establishments. By supporting local restaurants, you can help ensure the continued vibrancy and diversity of New York City's food scene. Consider dining at neighborhood eateries and independent restaurants, and tip generously to support the hardworking staff.

7.8: Iconic Restaurants to Try

No visit to New York City is complete without trying some of its iconic restaurants. Here are a few must-visit spots:

1 Katz's Delicatessen: This Lower East Side institution has been serving up pastrami sandwiches and other Jewish deli favorites since 1888. It's a bit of a tourist trap, but the food is worth the crowds.

2 Lombardi's Pizza: New York-style pizza is a thing, and Lombardi's is widely considered to be the originator. This Little Italy joint has been slinging coal-fired pies since 1905.

3 The Oyster Bar: Located in Grand Central Terminal, the Oyster Bar has been serving up fresh seafood for over a century. The decor is a bit old-school, but the oysters and other seafood are top-notch.

4 Peter Luger Steakhouse: For a classic steakhouse experience, head to Peter Luger in Brooklyn. The restaurant has been around since 1887 and is famous for its dry-aged beef.

5 Russ & Daughters: This Jewish deli on the Lower East Side has been a fixture in the neighborhood since 1914. It's famous for its smoked fish and bagels with lox and cream cheese.

7.9: Food Festivals and Events

Throughout the year, New York City hosts a variety of food festivals and events that are worth checking out. Some of the most popular include:

1 The New York City Wine & Food Festival: This annual event, which takes place in the fall, features celebrity chefs, food tastings, and wine seminars.

2 The Vendy Awards: This street food competition pits the city's best food trucks and carts against each other.

3 Smorgasburg: This weekly outdoor food market in Brooklyn features dozens of food vendors serving up everything from tacos to ice cream.

4 The New York City Hot Sauce Expo: For spice lovers, this annual event is a must-visit. It features hot sauce vendors from around the country, as well as spicy food challenges and eating contests.

New York City's food scene is vast and varied, with something for every taste and budget. By exploring different neighborhoods, trying new foods, and supporting local restaurants, you can have a memorable and delicious dining experience in the city.

In conclusion, dining out in New York City is a unique and exciting experience. By exploring different cuisines, making reservations in advance, navigating restaurant etiquette, and trying new foods, you can make the most of your dining experiences. Be sure to support local restaurants and enjoy all that the city's food scene has to offer.

Chapter 8: Culture and Entertainment: Making the Most of New York City's Art Scene

New York City is home to some of the world's most iconic museums, theaters, music venues, and cultural institutions. From Broadway shows to avant-garde art exhibits, there is no shortage of cultural experiences to be had in the city. In this chapter, we'll explore some of the best ways to immerse yourself in New York City's art and culture scene.

8.1: Museums and Art Galleries

New York City has a wealth of museums and art galleries, ranging from world-famous institutions like the Metropolitan Museum of Art and the Museum of Modern Art to small, independent galleries showcasing the work of emerging artists.

Here are a few must-visit spots:

1 The Metropolitan Museum of Art: Located on Fifth Avenue, the Met is one of the largest and most comprehensive art museums in the world. Its collection spans thousands of years of art and

includes everything from ancient Egyptian artifacts to contemporary paintings.

2 The Museum of Modern Art: Commonly known as MoMA, this Midtown museum is home to a wide range of modern and contemporary art. The collection includes works by famous artists like Jackson Pollock, Pablo Picasso, and Andy Warhol.

3 The Whitney Museum of American Art: Located in the Meatpacking District, the Whitney focuses on 20th and 21st-century American art. Its collection includes works by artists like Edward Hopper, Georgia O'Keeffe, and Alexander Calder.

4 The Guggenheim Museum: Designed by Frank Lloyd Wright, the Guggenheim is a work of art in itself. Its collection includes modern and contemporary art from around the world.

5 The New Museum: This Lower East Side museum focuses on contemporary art and emerging artists. Its exhibitions often push the boundaries of traditional art forms and explore new media and technology.

8.2: Theater and Performing Arts

New York City is home to Broadway, the epicenter of American theater. But beyond the bright lights of Times Square, there are also off-Broadway and off-

off-Broadway productions, as well as a vibrant performing arts scene.

Here are a few must-see shows and venues:

1 Broadway: With dozens of shows running at any given time, Broadway offers something for everyone. Whether you're into musicals, plays, or experimental theater, you're sure to find something that catches your interest.

2 Lincoln Center: Located on Manhattan's Upper West Side, Lincoln Center is home to the New York Philharmonic, the Metropolitan Opera, and the New York City Ballet. The campus also includes several theaters and outdoor performance spaces.

3 The Public Theater: This downtown theater is known for its innovative productions and commitment to promoting new voices in the performing arts. It's where Hamilton got its start before moving to Broadway.

4 BAM (Brooklyn Academy of Music): Located in Brooklyn, BAM is a cultural institution that hosts theater, dance, music, and film events throughout the year. The venue also includes a cafe and bar, making it a great spot to hang out before or after a show.

8.3: Music Venues

From jazz clubs to rock venues, New York City has a long and storied history of live music.

Here are a few venues worth checking out:

1 The Bowery Ballroom: Located on the Lower East Side, this intimate venue has hosted everyone from Adele to Arcade Fire. Its stage has a reputation for being a launchpad for up-and-coming acts.

2 The Village Vanguard: This iconic jazz club in Greenwich Village has been around since 1935 and has hosted some of the genre's biggest names. The dimly lit basement space has a cozy, intimate atmosphere that's perfect for enjoying live music.

3 Carnegie Hall: This Midtown concert venue is one of the most prestigious and historic music halls in the world. Since its opening in 1891, Carnegie Hall has hosted some of the most celebrated performers and ensembles in classical, jazz, and popular music.

4 Madison Square Garden: Known as "The World's Most Famous Arena," Madison Square Garden is a legendary venue that has hosted some of the biggest names in music. From Elvis Presley to Beyonce, this iconic arena is a must-visit for music fans.

8.4: Film and TV

New York City has been the backdrop for countless movies and TV shows, and there are plenty of ways to immerse yourself in the city's rich film and TV history.

Here are a few must-see spots:

1 The Museum of the Moving Image: Located in Astoria, Queens, the Museum of the Moving Image is dedicated to the art, history, and technology of film, television, and digital media. It includes a collection of artifacts, interactive exhibits, and screenings of classic films and TV shows.

2 The Film Forum: This Lower Manhattan theater screens independent and classic films. It also hosts Q&A sessions with filmmakers and actors.

3 NBC Studios: Located at Rockefeller Center, NBC Studios offers guided tours that take visitors behind the scenes of some of the network's most popular shows, including Saturday Night Live and The Tonight Show Starring Jimmy Fallon.

8.5: Festivals and Events

New York City is home to a wide variety of festivals and events throughout the year, celebrating everything from food to music to art.

Here are a few annual events to put on your calendar:

1 New York Fashion Week: Held twice a year, in February and September, Fashion Week is a chance to see the latest collections from some of the world's top designers.

2 The Tribeca Film Festival: Founded by Robert De Niro in the wake of 9/11, the Tribeca Film Festival showcases a mix of independent and mainstream films, as well as panel discussions and other events.

3 The Macy's Thanksgiving Day Parade: This iconic parade, which takes place on Thanksgiving Day, features larger-than-life balloons, floats, and performances from Broadway shows and marching bands.

4 The New York City Wine and Food Festival: Held in October, this foodie festival features tastings and demonstrations from some of the city's top chefs and restaurants.

In conclusion, New York City is a cultural and artistic hub that offers an abundance of experiences for anyone who wants to explore its vibrant and diverse cultural scene. By attending some of the city's museums, galleries, theaters, music venues, and festivals, you'll gain an appreciation for the art and culture that make New York City so unique.

Chapter 9: Health and wellness: staying healthy in the city

Living in New York City can be a fast-paced and exciting experience, but it can also be stressful and hectic. To maintain your overall health and well-being, it's important to prioritize your physical and mental health. This chapter will cover some tips and resources for staying healthy in the city.

9.1: Exercise

Staying active is important for your physical and mental health, and there are plenty of ways to get your heart rate up in New York City.

Some options include:

1 Running or walking in Central Park: With over 800 acres of green space, Central Park is the perfect place to get some fresh air and exercise. The park has several running and walking paths, as well as designated areas for sports like soccer and softball.

2 Taking a fitness class: New York City is home to a wide variety of fitness studios, from yoga and

Pilates to high-intensity interval training and dance classes.

3 Using a city park gym: The New York City Parks Department has installed several outdoor gyms throughout the city, complete with equipment for strength training and cardio.

9.2: Mental Health

The fast-paced and high-stress environment of New York City can take a toll on your mental health, so it's important to prioritize self-care and seek out resources when you need support.

Here are a few options:

1 Seeking therapy: New York City has a wealth of mental health professionals, and there are many different types of therapy available, from traditional talk therapy to more alternative methods like art therapy or hypnotherapy.

2 Practicing mindfulness: Mindfulness practices like meditation and yoga can help you manage stress and improve your overall well-being. There are many studios and classes available throughout the city.

3 Joining a support group: There are many support groups available in New York City for a variety of

issues, from addiction and mental health to grief and chronic illness.

9.3: Healthcare

New York City has a wide variety of healthcare resources, including hospitals, clinics, and private practices.

Here are a few things to keep in mind:

1 Finding a doctor: The New York State Department of Health has a website where you can search for licensed healthcare providers in the city.

2 Health insurance: If you don't have health insurance, you may be eligible for Medicaid or other low-cost healthcare options. The New York State of Health website can help you find the right coverage for your needs.

3 Emergency services: If you need emergency medical care, call 911 or go to the nearest emergency room. Many hospitals in New York City have emergency departments that are open 24/7.

9.4: Nutrition

New York City is known for its diverse and delicious food scene, but it can be challenging to maintain a healthy diet amid so many tempting options.

Here are some tips for eating well in the city:

Cook at home: Cooking your meals is a great way to control what you're eating and save money. There are many grocery stores and farmers' markets throughout the city.

1 Seek out healthy options: There are many restaurants and cafes in New York City that offer healthy and nutritious options, from smoothie bowls to salads and grain bowls.

2 Limit alcohol and caffeine: While it's tempting to indulge in a boozy brunch or a late-night espresso, excessive alcohol, and caffeine consumption can take a toll on your health. Try to limit your intake and prioritize water and other hydrating beverages.

In addition to physical health, mental health is also crucial for living in New York City. With the fast-paced lifestyle and constant hustle and bustle, it's important to take care of your mental well-being. Luckily, there are many resources available in the city to help you maintain your mental health.

One option is to seek therapy or counseling. There are many therapists and counseling services available in the city, and you can often find providers who specialize in specific areas of mental health, such as anxiety or depression. Additionally, many employers offer mental health benefits as part of their health insurance plans.

Another way to stay mentally and physically healthy is to prioritize self-care. This can include regular exercise, getting enough sleep, and taking time to do things you enjoy, such as reading or practicing a hobby.

New York City also offers many opportunities for spiritual and emotional growth. There are numerous religious institutions and spiritual communities throughout the city, as well as wellness centers and yoga studios that focus on mindfulness and meditation.

In conclusion, staying healthy in New York City requires some effort and intention, but there are many resources available to support your physical and mental well-being. By prioritizing exercise, mental health, healthcare, and nutrition, you can enjoy all that the city has to offer while maintaining a healthy and balanced lifestyle.

By prioritizing your mental and physical health, you can ensure that you're able to fully enjoy all that New York City has to offer.

Chapter 10: safety and security: staying safe in New York City

New York City is generally a safe place to live, but like any big city, there are certain precautions you should take to stay safe.

Here are some tips for staying safe in New York City:

1 Be aware of your surroundings: When you're out and about, pay attention to what's going on around you. Avoid walking with your phone out and keep your purse or bag close to your body.

2 Use public transportation safely: When using public transportation, be aware of your surroundings and keep an eye on your belongings. Try to avoid empty train cars and isolated subway platforms.

3 Lock your doors and windows: Make sure your apartment or house is secure by locking all doors and windows. If you live in a building with a doorman or security personnel, be sure to follow their procedures for entering and exiting the building.

4 Know your emergency contacts: Keep a list of emergency contacts, including the number for the police, fire department, and your building's management or security personnel. Make sure you know how to contact them in case of an emergency.

5 Avoid dangerous areas: Some parts of the city may be more dangerous than others, so be aware of where you're going and take precautions if you're in an unfamiliar area. Avoid walking alone at night in areas that are not well-lit or crowded.

6 Stay up to date on safety information: Keep up to date on safety information and alerts from local news sources and the city government. Familiarize yourself with emergency procedures and evacuation routes for your neighborhood.

7 Use common sense when socializing: When socializing in the city, be sure to use common sense and good judgment. Be cautious about accepting drinks from strangers or going to unfamiliar places alone. Always let someone know where you are going and who you will be with.

8 Be prepared for emergencies: It's important to be prepared for emergencies in New York City. Keep an emergency kit with basic supplies such as water, non-perishable food, a first aid kit, and a flashlight. Familiarize yourself with emergency

procedures for your building or neighborhood and be ready to evacuate if necessary.

9 Be cautious of scams and frauds: Unfortunately, scams and frauds can be common in the city. Be cautious of anyone who asks for your personal information or money, and never give out your social security number or other sensitive information. If something seems too good to be true, it probably is.

10 Report suspicious activity: If you see something suspicious or illegal, report it to the authorities. This can include anything from theft or assault to a potential terrorist threat. You can report suspicious activity to the police or by calling the city's 311 hotlines.

By taking these precautions and being aware of your surroundings, you can help ensure that you stay safe and secure while living in New York City. Remember, the city can be an exciting and vibrant place to live, but it's important to stay alert and prepared.

By following these safety tips, you can help ensure that you stay safe and secure while living in New York City.

Chapter 11 Building your social circle: meeting people and making

Friends in the city:

Moving to a new city can be exciting, but it can also be overwhelming, especially when it comes to meeting new people and making friends. In New York City, there are countless opportunities to build your social circle and make meaningful connections with others.

Here are some tips for meeting people and building a social network in the city:

1 Join clubs or groups: One of the best ways to meet new people is to join clubs or groups that align with your interests or hobbies. Whether it's a book club, a running group, or a volunteer organization, there are plenty of options in the city to connect with others who share your passions.

2 Attend events: New York City is home to countless events and activities, from festivals and concerts to lectures and workshops. Attend events that interest you and take the opportunity to strike up conversations with others.

3 Use social media: Social media can be a great tool for meeting new people in the city. Join local groups on Facebook or Meetup to connect with others who share your interests.

4 Take classes: Another way to meet people is to take classes or workshops in areas that interest you. This could include cooking, dance, art, or language classes.

5 Volunteer: Volunteering is not only a great way to give back to the community, but it's also a great way to meet new people and make connections with others who are passionate about making a difference.

6 Attend networking events: Networking events are a great way to meet new people and make professional connections. Attend industry-specific events or general networking events to connect with others in your field.

7 Explore your neighborhood: Take the time to explore your neighborhood and frequent local shops and restaurants. You may meet other residents who share your interests or hobbies.

8 Attend social events at work: If you work in New York City, attending social events organized by your workplace can be a great way to meet colleagues outside of the office and build professional relationships.

9 Use dating apps: Dating apps are a popular way to meet new people and make romantic connections. If you're single, consider using apps like Tinder, Bumble, or Hinge to connect with others in the city.

10 Attend community events: New York City is home to many community events, from block parties to street fairs. Attend these events and strike up conversations with those around you.

11 Join a gym: Joining a gym is a great way to stay healthy and also meet new people who are also interested in fitness. Many gyms also offer group classes and social events, which can be a great opportunity to connect with others.

12 Attend religious services: If you're religious, attending services at a local place of worship can be a great way to connect with others who share your beliefs and values.

Remember, building a social circle takes time and effort. Don't be discouraged if you don't make connections right away. Keep putting yourself out there and be open to meeting new people. Over time, you'll build a strong network of friends and acquaintances in the city.

Building a social circle takes time and effort, but it's important for your overall well-being and happiness.

By taking advantage of the many opportunities to connect with others in the city, you can build a strong network of friends and acquaintances who will support you and enrich your life.

Chapter 12: The future: Building a life in the city

New York City is a place where dreams are made, and people from all over the world come to make them a reality. As you settle into your life in the city, it's important to think about your future and how you can continue to grow and thrive.

1 Set long-term goals: Setting long-term goals is an essential part of building a life in New York City. Whether you want to advance in your career, buy a home, or start a family, having clear goals in mind can help you stay focused and motivated.

2 Invest in your education: New York City is home to some of the best colleges and universities in the world. If you're interested in furthering your education, consider enrolling in a program at one of these institutions. Whether it's earning an advanced degree or taking continuing education classes, investing in your education can help you reach your career goals and build a better future for yourself.

3 Build a professional network: Building a professional network is key to advancing in your career and achieving your long-term goals. Attend

networking events, join professional organizations, and connect with others in your industry. The more people you know, the more opportunities you'll have.

4 Save for the future: New York City can be an expensive place to live, and it's important to plan for your financial future. Set up a budget, save for emergencies, and start investing for the long term. Talk to a financial advisor to get guidance on how to best manage your finances.

5 Consider buying property: If you plan to stay in New York City for the long term, consider buying property. While the cost of living in the city can be high, property values also tend to appreciate over time, making it a sound investment. Talk to a real estate agent to learn more about the buying process and what you can afford.

6 Give back to your community: As you build your life in New York City, it's important to give back to your community. Volunteer at a local charity, donate to a cause you care about, or get involved in local politics. Building a better future for yourself also means building a better future for those around you.

7 Focus on personal growth: Building a life in the city is not just about professional success, but also personal growth. Take the time to pursue hobbies, travel, and explore the city. Join a sports league,

take an art class, or attend a cultural festival. The more you invest in your personal growth and happiness, the more successful and fulfilled you'll be in the long run.

8 Maintain a healthy work-life balance: It's easy to get caught up in the fast-paced lifestyle of New York City, but it's important to maintain a healthy work-life balance. Prioritize your personal life and take time to recharge and relax. Set boundaries with work and make time for friends, family, and hobbies.

9 Retirement plan: It's never too early to start planning for retirement. Talk to a financial advisor and start saving for the future. Consider investing in a retirement account or 401k plan, and make regular contributions. The earlier you start, the more time your money has to grow.

10 Embrace diversity: New York City is known for its diversity and multiculturalism. Embrace the city's melting pot of cultures and backgrounds, and seek out opportunities to learn about different traditions and perspectives. This will not only enrich your personal life but also help you build a more inclusive and diverse network.

11 Stay curious and keep learning: New York City is a hub of innovation and creativity, and there is always something new to discover. Stay curious and keep learning, whether it's through attending

lectures, taking classes, or exploring different neighborhoods. This will not only help you grow personally and professionally but also deepen your connection to the city.

12 Practice self-care: Finally, building a life in New York City can be stressful, and it's important to prioritize self-care. Make time for exercise, healthy eating, and relaxation. Seek out mental health resources if needed, and take care of yourself both physically and emotionally. By prioritizing self-care, you'll be better equipped to handle the challenges and opportunities that come your way.

New York City is a place of endless possibilities. By setting goals, building a professional network, and investing in your future, you can build a fulfilling and successful life in this vibrant and exciting city.

Building a life in New York City is a journey, and it takes time and effort to build a fulfilling and successful future. By setting goals, investing in your education and professional network, planning for the future, embracing diversity, and practicing self-care, you can create a life that is meaningful and rewarding. Remember to stay curious, stay connected, and always keep striving for growth and progress.

Conclusion:

Living in New York City can be both exciting and challenging, and it takes a lot of effort to navigate the complexities of the city. In this book, we've covered everything you need to know to thrive in the city, from finding an apartment to building a social circle and planning for the future.

By using the practical tips and advice outlined in each chapter, you can build a successful and fulfilling life in New York City. It's important to remember that building a life in the city takes time and effort, and it's not always easy. But with perseverance, determination, and a positive attitude, you can overcome any obstacle and achieve your goals.

Whether you're new to the city or have been living here for years, this book is a valuable resource for anyone looking to make the most of their time in New York City. By taking the knowledge and insights shared in this book and applying them to your own life, you can build a thriving career, create meaningful connections, and experience all that this vibrant and dynamic city has to offer. So get started on your New York City journey today, and embrace all the possibilities that lie ahead.

Printed in Great Britain
by Amazon

28058851R00056